Understanding A Company

The Basic Investor's Library

Chelsea House Publishers

Understanding
A Company

JEFFREY B. LITTLE

Paul A. Samuelson
Senior Editorial Consultant

CHELSEA HOUSE PUBLISHERS   New York   New Haven   Philadelphia

Editor-in-Chief   Nancy Toff
Executive Editor   Remmel T. Nunn
Managing Editor   Karyn Gullen Browne
Copy Chief   Juliann Barbato
Picture Editor   Adrian G. Allen
Art Director   Giannella Garrett
Manufacturing Manager   Gerald Levine

Staff for UNDERSTANDING A COMPANY
Senior Editor   Marjorie P. K. Weiser
Associate Editor   Andrea E. Reynolds
Assistant Editor   Karen Schimmel
Editorial Assistant   Tara P. Deal
Copyeditor   Michael Goodman
Associate Picture Editor   Juliette Dickstein
Picture Researcher   Johanna Cypis
Senior Designer   Laurie Jewell
Designers   Barbara Bachman, Ghila Krajzman
Production Coordinator   Joseph Romano

Creative Director   Harold Steinberg

Contributing Editor   Robert W. Wrubel
Consulting Editor   Shawn Patrick Burke

First Printing
1   3   5   7   9   8   6   4   2

Library of Congress Cataloging in Publication Data

Little, Jeffrey B.
   Understanding a company.

   (The Basic investor's library)
   Bibliography: p.
   Includes index.
   1. Financial statements—Juvenile literature.
2. Corporations—Finance—Juvenile literature.
[1. Corporations—Finance. 2. Financial statements]
I. Title. II. Series.
HG4028.B2L57   1988   657'.33   87-17654

ISBN 1-55546-622-2

CONTENTS

Learning the Tools of Investing

PAUL A. SAMUELSON

When asked why the great financial house of Morgan had been so successful, J. Pierpont Morgan replied, "Do you suppose that's because we take money seriously?"

Managing our personal finances is a serious business, and something we all must learn to do. We begin life dependent on someone else's income and capital. But after we become independent, it is a remorseless fact of nature that we must not only support ourselves for the present but must also start saving money for retirement. The best theory of saving that economists have is built upon this model of *life-cycle saving*: You must provide in the long years of prime working life for what modern medicine has lengthened to, potentially, decades of retirement. This life-cycle model won a 1985 Nobel Prize for my MIT colleague Franco Modigliani, and it points up the need to learn the rudiments of personal finance.

Learning to acquire wealth, however, is only part of the story. We must also learn to avoid losing what we have acquired. There is an old saying that "life insurance is *sold*, not bought." The same goes for stocks and bonds. In each case, the broker is guaranteed a profit, whether or not the customer benefits from the transaction. Knowledge is the customer's only true ally in the world of finance. Some gullible victims have lost their lifetime savings to unscrupulous sales promoters. One chap buys the Brooklyn Bridge. Another believes a stranger who asserts that gold will quickly double in price, with no risk of a drop in value. Such "con" (confidence) rackets get written up in the newspapers and on the police blotters every day.

I am concerned, however, about something less dramatic than con artists; something that is not at all illegal, but that costs ordinary citizens a thousand times more than outright embezzlement or fraud. Consider two families, neighbors who could be found in any town. They started alike. Each worked equally hard, and had about the same income. But the Smiths have to make do with half of what the Joneses have in retirement income, for one simple reason: The Joneses followed prudent practice as savers and investors, while the Smiths tried to make a killing and constantly bought and sold stocks at high commissions.

The point is, it does matter to learn how financial markets work, and how you can participate in them to your best advantage. It is important to know the difference between *common* and *preferred* stocks, between *convertible* and *zero-coupon* bonds. It is not difficult to find out what *mutual funds* are, and to understand the difference between the successful Fund A, which charges no commission, or "load," and the equally successful Fund B, which does charge the buyer such a fee.

All investing involves risk. When I was a young assistant professor, I said primly to my great Harvard teacher, Joseph Schumpeter: "We should speculate only with money we can afford to lose." He gently corrected me: "Paul, there is no such money. Besides, a speculator is merely an investor who has lost." Did Schumpeter exaggerate? Of course he did, but in the good cause of establishing the basic point of financial management: Good past performance is no guarantee of the future.

That is why *diversification* is the golden rule. "Don't put all your eggs in one basket. And watch all those baskets!" However, diversification does not mean throwing random darts at the financial pages of the newspaper to choose the best stocks in which to invest. The most diversified strategy of all would be to invest in a portfolio containing all the stocks in the comprehensive Standard & Poor's 500 Stock Index. But rather than throw random darts at the financial pages to pick out a few stocks, why not throw a large bath towel at the newspaper instead? Buy a bit of everything in proportion to its value in the larger world: Buy more General Motors than Ford, because GM is the bigger company; buy General Electric as well as GM because the auto industry is just one of many industries. That is called being an *index investor*. Index investing makes sense because 70 out of 100 investors who try to do better than the Standard & Poor's 500, the sober record shows, do worse over a 30-year period.

Do not take my word for this. The second lesson in finance is to be skeptical of what writers and other experts say, and that includes being skeptical of professors of economics. So I wish readers *Bon voyage!* on their cruise to command the fundamentals of investing. On your mainship flag, replace the motto "Nothing ventured, nothing gained" with the Latin words *Caveat emptor*—Let the buyer beware.

Understanding A Company

A n investor's best guide to how well a company is likely to perform in the future is how the company has performed in the past. A company whose stock has performed well over the past 10 or 20 years will usually have a superior record of earnings, dividends, and an improved financial condition over that period. Investors should also know exactly what a company does and how its business relates to the overall economy.

Investors will find it easier to identify superior companies once they understand some basic techniques of security analysis. This book will show you how to read a company's financial statements and follow its progress. It highlights the most important analytical concepts used by successful long-term investors.

GETTING TO KNOW THE COMPANY

What is this company's business? is the first question an investor should always ask. Investors must understand the kind of work a company does before they can begin to judge whether the company will be successful at what it does.

There are almost as many ways to organize a company as there are products and services for a company to create. Companies in different industries are organized in different ways. The operations of automobile manufacturers bear little resemblance to those of fast-food restaurant chains. Their goals and the arenas in which they compete are likewise dissimilar.

A worker at General Motors inspects a robot that applies a rust-preventing coating to trucks. Companies in the same industry are organized in similar ways.

Many important companies cannot be identified by a single type of product. One diversified company may produce, for example, motorbikes, golf clubs, tennis balls, and football helmets. In addition, there are large *conglomerates*, or combined companies, that operate businesses in many different lines.

Yet, like a ship, a company must have a charted course to follow. Companies express their goals in a statement such as "We manufacture and sell quality sporting goods for the leisure-time market." Before anything else, investors should know the corporate purpose and have confidence that the company's management also knows its purpose.

The organization of a fast-food restaurant chain is different from that of an automobile manufacturer.

But there are many other things a prospective investor will want to find out, and there are various ways to become acquainted with a company. These include materials provided by the company itself and reports about the company prepared for various purposes by outsiders.

Brokerage Reports

Large brokerage firms employ staffs of professional securities analysts. These people study thousands of companies to determine their potential as investments. Securities analysts specialize in companies within specific industries and follow industry trends as well. They regularly issue research reports that contain information and recommendations about companies they follow. Brokerage reports provide insight into a company's history, management, products, and competition, and make sophisticated assessments of its financial condition. These analyses are used by stockbrokers in the firm to make recommendations to customers. However, because brokerage firms gain by encouraging clients to make transactions that pay high commissions, investors should view such reports critically.

```
RESEARCH COMMENT:  1439
JUNE 9, 1987
  ROBERT I. ROTH

                    BEST PRODUCTS (BES-NYSE)
            FIRST QUARTER EARNINGS REVIEW - OUTLOOK

INTERMEDIATE TERM OPINION:  NEUTRAL (3)
LONG TERM OPINION:          NEUTRAL (3)

RECENT PRICE:  9 3/4                52 WEEK RANGE:  15 7/8 - 8 1/8

--FY JAN. EARNINGS PER SHARE*--    ---P/E RATIO--    IND. ANNUAL
1986        1987E       1988E      1987E    1988E    DIV. YIELD
$0.21**   $0.65-0.85  $0.90-1.10   13.0      9.8     NIL   ---

*FOR FISCAL YEARS ENDED JANUARY OF FOLLOWING CALENDAR YEAR.
**FROM CONTINUING OPERATIONS AND EXCLUDING EXTRAORDINARY CHARGES
FOR STORE CLOSINGS AND EARLY RETIREMENT OF DEBT.

SHARES OUTSTANDING:  27.1 MIL.    LT DEBT PC OF CAPITAL:   54PC
MARKET VALUE:        $265 MIL.    RETURN ON AVG E87 EQUITY: 5.2PC
BOOK VALUE:          $14.10 P/S   EST. 5 YR. EPS GROWTH:   10.5PC

SUITABILITY:        SPECULATIVE    INVEST. CHARACTER:  CYCLICAL
INDUSTRY CLASS:  MDSG.-SPECIALTY   OPTIONS:  NONE

SUMMARY:
    BEST REALIZED A FAVORABLY REDUCED YEAR-TO-YEAR NET LOSS IN THE
SEASONALLY SMALL FIRST QUARTER, AGAINST A DEPRESSED YEAR-EARLIER
PERFORMANCE, AS IMPORTANTLY BOLSTERED BY IMPROVED PRETAX OPERATING
MARGINS.  MORE SPECIFICALLY, THE NET LOSS FROM CONTINUING
OPERATIONS FAVORABLY DECLINED BY 20.0PC TO $0.24 PER SHARE FROM
$0.30 PER SHARE (EXCLUDING THE DISPOSED 17 UNPROFITABLE CATALOG
SHOWROOMS AS WELL AS THE UNPROFITABLE 33-STORE ASHBY'S APPAREL
CHAIN) IN THE FIRST QUARTER OF 1986 (REPORTED FIRST QUARTER 1986
NET LOSS OF $0.35 PER SHARE INCLUDING THE DISCONTINUED
OPERATIONS).  THE FIRST QUARTER PRETAX MARGIN IMPROVEMENT, AGAINST
WEAK YEAR-EARLIER RESULTS, OCCURRED NOTWITHSTANDING CONTINUED
BELOW-BUDGET SALES.  THE PRIMARY PRETAX MARGIN IMPROVEMENT ONCE
AGAIN OCCURRED AT THE GROSS MARGIN LEVEL.  WHILE THE SELLING,
GENERAL AND ADMINISTRATIVE EXPENSE-SALES RATIO DECLINED MODERATELY,
AGAINST A WEAK PRIOR-YEAR PERFORMANCE, DESPITE BELOW-BUDGET SALES
(SAME-STORE SALES DECLINE OF 4.4PC IN THE FIRST QUARTER COMPARED
WITH A BELOW-BUDGET 2.2PC SAME-STORE SALES DECLINE IN THE
PRIOR-YEAR PERIOD).  SLIGHTLY RESTRICTING THE FIRST QUARTER
EARNINGS IMPROVEMENT WAS AN UNFAVORABLE DECLINE IN THE TAX CREDIT
RATE TO 45.80PC FROM THE PRIOR-YEAR 47.40PC TAX CREDIT RATE.  THE
ACQUISITIONS OF MODERN AND BASCO HAVE OBVIOUSLY BROADENED BEST'S
ALREADY CONSIDERABLE OPERATING LEVERAGE AND THEREBY REINFORCE OUR
SPECULATIVE (3) SUITABILITY RATING ON THE COMPANY'S COMMON SHARES.
CORRESPONDINGLY, THE ACQUISITIONS, TOGETHER WITH AN EXTENSIVE
(MORE)
```

The first page of a quarterly research report analyzing a retail company. Such reports are used by brokers to recommend stock transactions to clients.

Investors should read brokerage reports for the factual information they contain but should pay less attention to conjectural statements. An investment decision should be made by the investor on the basis of all information available, not under pressure from a broker.

Independent Research Organization Analyses

There are a number of large, well-respected organizations whose sole business is to gather data on the performance of thousands of companies. These organizations present the data in ways that permit investors to compare key aspects of large groups of stocks. Two of the best known among these standard financial services are Standard & Poor's Corporation and Moody's Investors Service. Publications from both organizations are available at brokerage offices and many libraries. Moody's publishes six annual manuals that contain summaries of past financial statements and other information about major companies in different industries, as well as monthly stock and bond surveys. Standard & Poor's publishes various stock and bond guides, a survey of bond material activity called *Credit Week*, and the *Standard Corporation Records*. The latter publication is issued regularly in looseleaf form, and it contains such information as 10-year histories of sales, earnings, assets, and liabilities of many major companies.

Moody's Investors Service publishes several directories containing data about industrial and other companies.

Company-Provided Literature

By law, publicly held companies must issue to stockholders (and anyone else who asks) detailed statements about aspects of their operations that affect the value of their stocks. This information is presented in such company literature as the prospectus, annual reports, and quarterly statements. Other information provided by a company may be found in speeches given by top managers, advertisements, and press releases. A prospectus, annual or quarterly reports, and press releases can be obtained free of charge by writing to the secretary or public relations office of the corporation. The company's mailing address may be found on its products, at any brokerage office, or in reference books available at public libraries, such as the *Standard & Poor's Register*, which also gives the names of corporate secretaries and telephone numbers for about 45,000 corporations.

Standard & Poor's publishes surveys and directories containing financial data for thousands of corporations.

Annual Meetings

Publicly held companies are required by law to convene a meeting for all shareholders every year. At the annual meeting, the company's managers give a presentation that covers the financial results and important events of the past year, as well as plans for the future. Shareholders may ask questions about company performance and policy and exercise their voting rights as part owners in the enterprise.

The meeting is usually held at or near the corporate headquarters, although many large, widely owned companies accommodate stockholders by holding their annual meetings in a different city each year. In most cases, the annual meeting is scheduled for about the same day every year, according to the company's bylaws. The date, time, and location of the annual meeting are usually noted on the inside cover of the annual report. Investment industry reference works, available at a brokerage firm or public library, can also provide this information.

A major order of business at an annual meeting is the election of the company's directors by the stockholders. Each stockholder usually has one vote for every share of stock owned. Thus each has an influence in proportion to his or her investment in the company. Many, perhaps most, shareholders do not cast their votes at the annual meeting itself. Several weeks before the meeting, the company mails a *proxy statement* to each shareholder. The statement announces any votes to be taken at the annual meeting. If directors are to be elected, a brief biography of each candidate is included. Each investor can review the material included in the mailing and decide how to vote in the election of directors and on other proposals. The stockholder can then fill out a proxy ballot card and mail it back to the company. It will be counted with other bal-

The company sends every stockholder a notice of its annual meeting, including the agenda and information about votes to be taken.

Companies publish annual reports to inform investors of company performance during the past year.

Proxy ballots are mailed to shareholders so that those who cannot attend the annual meeting are able to vote on issues concerning the company.

INVESTORS MUTUAL, INC., MINNEAPOLIS, MINNESOTA
THIS PROXY IS SOLICITED ON BEHALF OF MANAGEMENT

The undersigned shareholder of Investors Mutual, Inc. (the Fund) hereby appoints Robert S. Ersted and William C. Herber, or either of them (with full power to act without the other) the attorney and proxy of the undersigned, with full power of substitution, to vote all of the shares of the Fund standing in the name of the undersigned with all of the powers, including the power to vote for the election of directors and to cumulate votes for any of the nominees for director (Check here if you wish to withhold authority to vote for directors ☑), which the undersigned would possess if personally present at the Annual Meeting of shareholders of the Fund to be held at the Multifoods Building, Minneapolis, Minnesota on July 13, 1977, and any adjournment thereof. All proxies heretofore given to vote at such meeting are hereby revoked. **Management recommends a vote FOR the proposals.** The proxy is authorized to vote as specified below upon the following proposals:

FOR AGAINST

☐ ☐ (a) Approval of a proposal which will allow accounts with less than $300 to be redeemed. (Proposal 2)

☐ ☐ (b) Approval of a proposal for the Fund to write call options. (Proposal 3)

☐ ☐ (c) Ratification of the selection of Peat, Marwick, Mitchell & Co. as independent public accountants. (Proposal 4)

☐ ☐ (d) Approval of a change in the Custodian Agreement. (Proposal 5)

The Undersigned's vote will be cast in the election of directors, unless such authority has been withheld, and FOR the proposals on the reverse side unless otherwise indicated. Discretionary authority is hereby conferred for other matters as may properly arise at the meeting.

SIGN HERE *Betty M. Dornheim* BE SURE TO DATE 6/9/77

PLEASE DATE AND SIGN EXACTLY AS OWNER APPEARS BELOW • GUARDIAN OR PARENT MUST SIGN FOR MINORS. EXECUTORS, ADMINISTRATORS, TRUSTEES, ETC. SHOULD SO INDICATE.

0107-1364,417-6 BETTY M DORNHEIM
                 15 HAMILTON AVE   70
  4680370   BRONXVILLE N.Y. 10708   S 122 40666

4680370

NOTE If you do not intend to be at the meeting in person, please fill in and sign this proxy and mail at once in the enclosed envelope.

Stockholders must sign and return a proxy ballot.

lots cast at the annual meeting. Many shareholders—especially those who do not have the time or a large enough investment in the company to justify traveling to an annual meeting—will choose to vote by proxy. This means that another shareholder present at the meeting, usually an officer of the company, will represent them, casting their ballots as indicated on the proxy card.

Annual meetings can be interesting because the perspectives of investors and directors or executives of a company are quite different. Corporate executives who give presentations are of course working to make a favorable

General Motors, known throughout the world for its automobiles, also has a reputation for holding stimulating annual meetings.

impression. Investors, who are the owners of the company, are trying to look beneath smooth (or clumsy) presentations for signs of management talent (or weakness). Company presentations become increasingly valuable as an investor gains experience with different companies.

The business portion of the annual meeting usually takes a short time, but it can continue for more than an hour to accommodate the stockholders' question and answer period. Sometimes an annual meeting includes a tour of the company's offices or factories. Several companies, such as the Polaroid Corporation, General Motors Corporation, Texaco Inc., and others, are known for their stimulating annual meetings. If they can possibly attend, investors will find an annual meeting to be an interesting and worthwhile experience.

UNDERSTANDING FINANCIAL STATEMENTS

E very publicly owned company must prepare a variety of statements reviewing the year's financial results. These are combined in the annual report, which must be made available to all current and potential shareholders. Annual reports are usually issued following the end of each year of company operations, known as the *fiscal year*.

In most cases the fiscal year coincides with the calendar year, and thus the financial information given in most annual reports is as of December 31 of the preceding year. Reading an annual report is the best way to begin an analysis of a company.

What's in an Annual Report?

An annual report consists of three or four main sections. It starts off with the chairman's or president's letter to shareholders, which notes important events of the past year and outlines the present status of the corporation. The body of the annual report explains the company's business operations in greater detail. Often this section is presented in an easy-to-read narrative style, illustrated with photographs and charts. It may describe new products or new directors or discuss factory closings. It may explain how the company intends to respond to new government regulations, or it may hail the accomplishments of a retiring executive. Following this is a section called management's discussion of financial results, or financial review. This is a detailed interpretation, from the point of view of the company's management, of its financial activities and results. The topics for discussion include profits, borrowing, investments, and important events in the industry in general.

The Financial Section

The end of the annual report is its most revealing part—the financial section. The content of this section is determined by regulations of the Securities and Exchange Commission (SEC), a federal agency created in 1934 to regulate the investment industry. The financial section contains three important financial statements: the income statement, the balance sheet, and the source and application of funds statement. It may contain additional important data in the form of charts or notes and always includes an auditor's report.

The Income Statement   The *income statement* presents the company's business results for the year. It contains a column of numbers showing, in dollar terms, the company's sales, costs, and earnings (profits or income) over the past 12 months. Another column shows the same categories in the preceding 12-month period. Similar data may be shown for several earlier fiscal years as well.

The Balance Sheet   The *balance sheet* is a "snapshot" of the company's financial condition taken at a single moment at the end of the fiscal year. It shows where the company stands financially as a result of the data appearing on the income statement. The balance sheet lists the following:

1. *Assets*, or what the company owns (such as cash on hand, inventory, factories, land, equipment, etc.), and *receivables* (money due from customers).
2. *Liabilities*, or what the company owes (short-term borrowing and long-term debt), and *payables* (money owed to suppliers).
3. *Stockholders' equity*, or the value of the company (assets minus liabilities).

The Source and Application of Funds Statement   The *source and application of funds statement* is also known as *sources and uses* and may be headed "Changes in Financial Position Statement." It is best described as a bridge between the income statement and the balance sheet. It explains exactly how the company's financial position changed during the past year, or how the year's income and spending affected the year-end snapshot of the company's assets and liabilities. The source of funds section (which may also be headed "Cash Provided" or "Source of Working Capital") explains how the money used to finance the company's operations and growth during the year was obtained. The application of funds section (which may be headed "Investing and Financing Activities" or "Use of Working Capital") details how the money was spent.

Notes or Comments All three financial statements are accompanied by a series of notes (or footnotes) that explain some of the data in greater detail. Sometimes the notes, which may also be called comments, contain significant information. The notes always explain details about the operation of the company and its business activities.

Financial Summary or Highlights A table called *financial highlights* or *summary of financial data*, showing several years of financial history, is also included in the annual report. The table presents financial data that the company's managers believe are particularly important or impressive. It may cover 3, 5, or 10 years and often appears first in the annual report. By using the table, investors can observe the long-term progress of the company at a glance: Have sales been up every year? Have profits become greater over the years? How does stockholders' equity this year compare with that of last year?

Auditor's Report Finally, the financial section of the annual report of a publicly owned company must contain an *auditor's report*. The auditor is an independent accountant (an individual or an accounting firm not affiliated with the company) who reviews the company's financial data. This report, usually written as a letter, states that the company's financial statements were prepared in accordance with the standard accounting procedures used by all publicly owned companies. This analysis is required so that investors can be certain that the financial statements present a fair and consistent disclosure of the fiscal position of the company for the years noted. Investors should always read the auditor's report to check for any problems. A possible problem is sometimes referred to as a "qualification" in the auditor's report.

HOW TO READ A FINANCIAL STATEMENT

How the three financial statements in an annual report are constructed, how they relate to one another, and the fundamental story they tell can be shown in the example of the hypothetical, well-managed XYZ Company. The income statement, balance sheet, and source and application of funds statement of the XYZ Company are shown on pages 23, 26, and 29.

The most effective means of analyzing a company is to study its current operating and financial records and those that reflect the performance of the past few years. Then compare these records to those of other presumably well-managed companies that are in the same industry or have similar financial characteristics. It is important to compare companies in the same industry because such companies have many aspects of their operation in common. They sell

The financial data of companies in such dissimilar fields as pharmaceuticals and airlines cannot be compared, because different industries operate in different environments.

to the same market, for example, and must abide by the same government regulations; they hire workers with similar skills and experience; use the same raw materials; require similar means of transportation; and so on. Thus pharmaceutical manufacturers and airlines would not be comparable. Nor would retail chains be comparable to motion picture distributors.

All companies and their managements, however, have one thing in common that is very important, and that is the obligation to achieve the best possible investment return for the owners of the business (the stockholders). This almost always means making the best possible profit for the longest possible period of time.

An investor who buys a share of stock is acquiring a share of ownership in the company. The investor becomes a part owner of the company's *equity* or dollar value. The equity of the company is entrusted to the company's management. Management has the obligation to use this money wisely in order to obtain the best performance for shareholders. To do this, management must consider, among other factors, the company's business opportunities, its areas of expertise, and the degree of risk the stockholders are willing to assume.

Reading an Income Statement

The heading "Revenues" describes the total amount in dollars received by a company in a year. The greatest figure under this heading usually represents *sales to customers* and reflects the amount customers paid to the company for its products or services in the preceding year. XYZ Company sold $2,225,000 worth of its product last year. Many companies keep some of their funds in bank accounts or other investments and therefore earn *interest income*. They may hold patents on manufacturing processes or equipment, which they rent to other companies for a fee called a *royalty*. The sum of all revenue categories is *total revenues*.

The heading "Costs and Expenses" describes the various expenditures of the company in a year. The largest figure under this heading usually refers to the *cost of goods sold* (CGS) or *cost of sales*, which is the amount spent to produce the company's products. This figure includes expenditures for raw materials, wages, salaries, fuel, and other production-related costs. The XYZ Company paid $1,100,000 to manufacture and distribute its products last year.

XYZ COMPANY	
Income Statement For the year ended December 31	
(in thousands of dollars, except per share data)	
Revenues	
Sales to customers	$2,225
Interest income	12
Royalty and other income	15
Total revenues	$2,252
Costs and expenses	
Cost of Goods Sold	1,100
Selling, general and administrative expenses	755
Depreciation	69
Other expenses	18
Total costs and expenses	$1,942
Income before taxes	310
United States, foreign, and other income taxes	126
Net income	$ 184
Per share data	
Number of shares outstanding	200,000
Net income per share	$ .92
Dividends per share	$ .25

Selling, general, and administrative expenses (SG&AE) include officers' salaries, commissions paid to sales representatives, advertising costs, research and development

costs, and other general expenses. Costs of products sold plus SG&AE constitute the *total operating expenses.* For XYZ this would be $1,100,000 + $755,000 = $1,855,000.

The term *depreciation* refers to the decline in value of assets over a limited period of time. The assets that depreciate in value are usually property that is of greatest value when new, such as buildings and equipment. Such assets are typically used for quite a few years. Depreciation is a noncash source of income. Although it is not an outlay of money, it is considered an expense incurred while operating the business because it reflects the declining value of property as it is "used up." For example, a machine for making tennis shoes may have a 10-year service life. When it has been in use for five years, it is not worth the same amount as a new machine because it has already produced half the total number of shoes it will produce over its service lifetime. The *total costs and expenses* is the last item in this part of the table.

Once the revenues and expenditures are itemized, the profits can be figured. There are several kinds of profits. *Gross profits* are simply the difference between the company's revenues from sales and costs of sales. For the XYZ Company, this would be $2,225,000 − $1,100,000 = $1,125,000. The *operating profit* represents what is left of all earnings from the company's business activities minus expenditures. It is figured by subtracting the cost of sales, SG&AE, and depreciation from the sales revenues. Operating profit, in other words, does not consider revenues or expenses unrelated to the company's production and sales.

Earnings before taxes is the excess of total revenues over total costs and expenses before any taxes are paid by the company. The company's taxes are figured and then are subtracted from the earnings to determine the after-tax profit, or *net profit* (also called net income or net earnings).

The income statement usually also shows information about shares of its stock. These figures are of particular interest to shareholders. The number of shares outstanding is the number of shares of stock owned by stockholders. The net income per share is calculated by dividing the net income of the company in the preceding year by the number of shares outstanding. For XYZ, net income per share was $.92 last year. The company declared a dividend of $.25 per share.

Reading a Balance Sheet

The balance sheet is divided into three major parts: *assets*, or what the company owns; *liabilities*, or what the company owes; and *stockholders' equity*, or assets minus liabilities. Assets and liabilities are *long term* if they refer to any time period beyond 12 months. *Plant and equipment* is a typical long-term category of asset. Footnotes in the annual report may explain the nature of long-term assets and liabilities in greater detail; in the case of liabilities, the footnotes will indicate when the debts are to be repaid. *Current assets* are *liquid*; that is, they will most likely be converted to cash within 12 months. *Current liabilities* are obligations that will be paid within 12 months.

Among the items included in current assets, in addition to cash and marketable securities (stocks and bonds owned by the company), are *accounts receivable* and *inventories*. Accounts receivable consists of money owed to the company by customers. Inventories are raw materials, work in process, supplies, and finished products ready to be sold.

Current liabilities begins with *accounts payable*, which represents the money the company owes to suppliers of raw materials, office supplies, and various services needed in the normal course of business. *Loans and notes payable*

XYZ COMPANY		
Balance Sheet for the year ended December 31		
(in thousands of dollars)		

Assets		**Liabilities and Stockholders' Equity**	
Current assets			
Cash	$ 38	**Current liabilities**	
Marketable securities	200	Accounts payable	$ 99
Accounts receivable	288	Loans and notes payable	88
Inventories	397	Other current liabilities	129
Other current assets	23		
Total Current Assets	946	**Total Current Liabilities**	316
		Long-term Debt	85
Long-term Assets		**Stockholders' equity**	
Property, plant, and equipment	528	Common stock	145
Other assets	77	Retained earnings	1,005
Total Long-term Assets	605	**Total Stockholders' Equity**	$1,150
Total Assets	$1,551	**Total Liabilities and Stockholders' Equity**	$1,551

represents debts that the company is obligated to pay, often to a bank or a supplier, within 12 months.

The excess of current assets over current liabilities represents a company's *working capital*. This is the amount of money a company can actually use to operate its business within the next 12 months. The XYZ Company has working capital of $630,000 ($946,000 in current assets minus $316,000 in current liabilities). Sometimes current liabilities may exceed current assets, although this will rarely happen with well-managed companies. When this situation does occur, the company is said to have *negative working capital*.

Stockholders' equity, or *net worth*, represents the holders' interest in the company and is defined as total assets minus total liabilities. It typically consists of two categories: *Common stock* represents the money the company received from shareholders in the sale of its stock. *Retained earnings* represents all the income reinvested in the company for the next year's operations. For XYZ, the total of common stock ($145,000) and retained earnings ($1,005,000) is $1,150,000. This is the stockholders' equity, the net worth of the company.

It is possible to figure out the amount of equity behind each share of common stock by dividing the amount of stockholders' equity by the number of shares of stock outstanding. This figure is known as *book value*. Let us suppose XYZ has 200,000 shares outstanding. Each share of XYZ stock is backed by a book value of $5.75 ($1,150,000 divided by 200,000).

In addition to common stock, many companies issue *preferred stock*. Holders of preferred stock get paid before owners of common stock when dividends are paid out or if the company becomes bankrupt and is forced to sell its assets. If there is preferred stock outstanding (though there is not in the XYZ Company), any money to which preferred shareholders are entitled must be deducted from the total stockholders' equity before the book value of the common stock can be calculated.

The term *par value* is frequently applied to common stock. Par value is an arbitrary amount put on a stock certificate and has no relation to the market price of the stock at any time. Values may be *no-par* or 15 cents or anything else. The term exists principally for internal bookkeeping purposes. Some states charge an incorporation fee based

on the par value of stocks being issued. For this reason, many companies place a low par value on their stock to keep the fee low. For preferred stock, on the other hand, par value may represent the price of the stock at the time it was issued. But no-par preferred stock is also issued. Sometimes preferred stocks pay a fixed dividend rate to shareholders. In that case, dividend payments may be fixed as a percent of the par. For example, an 11 percent dividend rate on $100 par would call for payment of $11 per share per year.

Reading a Source and Application of Funds Statement

The source and application of funds (sources and uses, or changes in financial position) statement provides a great deal of information about the actual working of the company. The source of funds information represents the actual cash income received by the company from various sources. Certain items on the income statement do not represent actual cash outlays. For example, depreciation expense is considered a source of funds. This is because, although it represents the estimated cost of using equipment or buildings, it is not an actual expense for which the company must pay cash.

The XYZ Company had several other sources of income, including an increase in long-term debt (it took out a bank loan); proceeds from employees' stock options (employees exercised their rights to purchase stock reserved for them); and proceeds from the sale of property (the company sold some land and a small building it no longer needed). These monies were not derived from the direct business operations of the company and hence are known as outside sources.

XYZ COMPANY

Source and Application of Funds Statement For
the year ended December 31

(in thousands of dollars)

Source of Funds

Net income	$184
Depreciation of property	69
Other sources	7
Total funds provided by current operations	260
Increase in long-term debt	13
Exercise of stock options	4
Sale of property	3
Total funds provided by outside sources	20
Total source of working capital	$280

Application of Funds

Expenditures of property, plant, and equipment	$135
Cash dividends paid	50
Decrease in long-term debt	10
Other	10
Total use of working capital	$205
Increase in working capital	$ 75

Application of funds refers to the ways in which the company used money, aside from the costs of doing business, which were reflected under costs and expenses in the income statement. The XYZ Company expanded its property and acquired some new equipment; paid dividends to shareholders; paid off some long-term debts; and had some other nonbusiness related expenses.

The excess of sources over uses for XYZ this year is $75,000, which is considered to be money that can be put back into the business, or an increase in working capital.

Other Important Calculations

There are many statistical calculations that seasoned investors use to analyze a company's financial situation. Here are some of the most important computations, based on figures provided in the preceding financial statements of the XYZ Company. (It will be helpful if you use a calculator to follow the examples given. In our calculations, decimals have been rounded to the nearest cent, dollar, or percent, as appropriate.)

Return on Equity   One of the most important calculations in determining whether management is doing a good job for the company's shareholders is *return on equity (ROE)*. This is a ratio that relates a company's net income to its stockholders' equity. The ROE indicates the rate of investment return the company's executives have been able to achieve with the equity entrusted to them. A return of much less than 10 percent is generally regarded as unsatisfactory. The return on equity is calculated by dividing

THE PROFITABILITY OF SELECTED INDUSTRIES						
Industry	**%ROE**	**Industry**	**%ROE**	**Industry**	**%ROE**
Aerospace	13.4	Computer Hardware	11.7	Household Appliances	15.9
Airlines	5.4	Computer Software	15.4	Insurance	7.1
Automotive	16.9	Discount/Variety Stores	13.5	Lumber and Wood Products	7.3
Broadcasting	9.6	Drugs	19.5	Machinery	3.1
Chemicals	6.5	Food Retailing	13.7	Textiles	9.8

Source: Sumner N. Levine, ed., *Business and Investment Almanac* (Homewood, IL: Dow-Jones-Irwin, 1987), pp. 45–134 passim.

the net earnings by the stockholders' equity. Our calculation will use the figures from XYZ's income statement (page 23) and balance sheet (page 26).

net earnings ÷ stockholders' equity = return on equity

$184,000 ÷ $1,150,000   =   16%

Investors often use the average equity over the past year for this computation, however, because the equity figure given on the balance sheet is a snapshot taken only at year-end, whereas the net earnings figure on the income statement represents income throughout the preceding 12 months. Stockholders' equity can vary significantly from one financial reporting period to another. Average equity is determined by averaging the equity at the beginning and end of the year.

Return on Total Assets   Using ROE alone can produce misleading results. For example, a poorly managed company can still achieve a high return on equity simply by showing a profit while having a low amount of equity (perhaps as the result of several unprofitable years) or by accumulating debts. For this reason, investors should calculate the company's *return on total assets* as well. This calculation is also known as *return on capital* because it answers the question of how much the company earns on the capital it uses. To find return on capital, divide the net income by the total assets.

net income ÷ total assets = return on capital

$184,000 ÷ $1,551,000 =   12%

When both return on equity and return on assets are high (10 percent or more), the company is considered to have good potential for growth and earnings.

Retention Rate   Another important calculation is the *retention rate* or percent of a company's net earnings reinvested into the business instead of being paid out in

dividends to investors. The retention rate is calculated from information found in the source and application of funds statement, and the formula is expressed as

net earnings − dividends ÷ net earnings = retention rate

XYZ Company distributed $50,000 of its $184,000 net income to stockholders in the form of dividends and put back the remaining income, $134,000, into the company to help expand operations. For XYZ the calculation of retention rate is

$184,000 − $50,000 = $134,000 ÷ $184,000 = 0.73 or 73%

The retention rate of a company is influenced directly by its dividend policy, and it can be adjusted at will by management merely by distributing more or less of the net earnings to investors. A company that grows entirely by reinvesting its earnings in the business is said to be self-financing. That is, it is using 100 percent of internally generated cash for capital expenditures. Generally speaking, the most successful companies today are self-financing because they do not have to rely on outside sources of money such as banks or other lenders. Being self-financing does not mean that the company pays no dividends.

Reinvestment Rate   Retention rate and return on equity are important calculations for investors and analysts because they give a clue to the company's *internal growth rate potential*. There are only two ways in which a company can acquire money for growth: by plowing its own net earnings back into its business or by obtaining new debt or equity capital from outside the company. Analysts calculate a company's growth potential by multiplying the return on equity by the retention rate to get the *reinvestment rate*.

The internal growth potential of the XYZ Company is therefore expressed as

return on equity × retention rate = reinvestment rate

16% × 73% = 11.7%

A company can improve its reinvestment rate by increasing either its return on equity or its retention rate or both. For example, if XYZ raised its return on equity to 20 percent and its retention rate to 80 percent, its reinvestment rate would go up to 16 percent.

Profit Margins   Profit margins are a very useful way to understand the percentage of a company's sales that becomes profits at various levels of the company's income statement. There are several different ways of figuring profit margin. The *operating profit margin* reflects the relationship of before-tax, or operating, profits to income from sales. This calculation tells an investor how profitable the company's products are to manufacture and sell.

operating profits ÷ sales = operating profit margin

$310,000 ÷ $2,225,000 = 13.9%

An operating profit margin of less than 8 percent is usually regarded as unsatisfactory for a manufacturing company. XYZ's operating profit margin of 13.9 percent is considered fairly healthy.

The *pretax profit margin*, or simply *pretax margin*, shows how profitable the company's operations have been from all sources of income, considering all costs except taxes. It is calculated this way:

operating profits ÷ total revenues = pretax profit margin

$310,000 ÷ $2,252,000 = 13.8%

(*continued on page 36*)

Analyzing McDonald's

Research analysts are employed by brokerage houses to study a particular industry and certain selected companies within that industry. Their purpose is to advise brokers in their firm about stocks to recommend to their customers. A typical research department at a large brokerage house may employ 30 analysts, each studying a different segment of the economy. One may study the steel industry, another electronics companies, and still another fast-food restaurant companies. By concentrating on one industry, the analyst develops contacts and expertise that would be impossible for the individual investor or broker to achieve.

To communicate their findings to stockbrokers who work for the brokerage house and to their potential clients, analysts write reports about the companies and industries they follow. In these reports they note recent activities of the company, predict future performance, and advise investors whether to buy, hold, or sell its stock.

Here are excerpts from a typical research report. An analyst who follows the fast-food industry is commenting on the performance of McDonald's Corp., after its first quarter of operations for the 1987 fiscal year. This analyst writes similar reports about several companies in this industry on a regular basis. The report starts by summarizing several important measures of performance:

o Quality of first-quarter earnings very high.
o Operating earnings jumped 23%. Capital gains fell 48%.
o Real growth at company stores up an estimated 1.5% domestically.

Next comes a table listing key financial data:

Earnings Per Share Fiscal Year Ending		P/E	Ind.		Opinion		Shares O/S	52- Week
12/86	12/87E	1987E	Div.	Yield	N	L	(mil.)	Range
$3.73	$4.25	18.6X	$0.66	0.8%	2	2	126.7	84-61

These numbers quickly convey information about the stock in relationship to the company's fiscal performance. Under the heading "Earnings Per Share," real earnings are shown for the end of the last fiscal year, and estimated earnings, marked "E," for the next year. The column headed "P/E" gives the price/earnings ratio or multiple (price of the stock divided by earnings per share as estimated) for the current fiscal year (1987E). No one can know yet what a company's actual performance for the year will be, but in their reports, analysts use computers to help them project an estimate of earnings and profits from operations. Other columns announce the dividend per share (Ind. Div.) and the yield as a percent of current stock price. The columns headed "Opinion" are explained by a key at the bottom of the first page of the report:

Opinion Legend: N = Up to 6 Months, L = 6 to 18 Months
1 = Aggressive Purchase, 2 = Accumulate, 3 = Average Performer
4 = Swap, 5 = Sell

Thus, the short-term (N, or near) and long-term (L) advice is for shareholders to accumulate (2), or buy and hold on to, stock in McDonald's Corp. Finally, there are columns showing the number of shares outstanding (O/S) in millions, and the high and low prices at which the stock traded in the 52 weeks before the date of the report.

An analyst's report often consists of two or more pages with tables like these, along with several paragraphs describing some of the data in greater detail. The remainder of the report summarizes the analyst's opinions about the company and its position in the fast-food industry. Some of the descriptive material is complex. But many of the analytical concepts discussed in this book are referred to throughout the report. You can see analysts' reports at a brokerage firm. Ask for one on a company that interests you.

(continued from page 33)

XYZ's 13.8 percent pretax profit margin is a healthy one.

Net profit margin can also be calculated from information given on the income statement. The net profit margin is the most important of the three profit margins because it measures a company's profitability after all costs and expenses, including taxes, have been paid. The percentage of net profit is figured by dividing net earnings (just above the per share data on the income statement) by total revenues:

net earnings ÷ total revenues = net profit margin

$184,000 ÷ $2,252,000 = 8.2%

A high net profit margin means that a company is managing to turn a good percentage of its sales into net income. For U.S. companies, 5 to 6 percent has been typical in recent years. However, typical rates vary considerably from one industry to another. For instance, a large supermarket chain is doing well if its net profit margin is 1 percent (that is, $1,000,000 in sales would produce $10,000 profit).

Although most U.S. companies have net profit margins between 5 and 6%, a rate of 1% is considered healthy in the supermarket industry.

Current Relationships   Two key measures of a company's financial health are calculated from information found on the balance sheet. *Current ratio* indicates the relationship between current assets and current liabilities.

current assets ÷ current liabilities = current ratio

$946,000   ÷ $316,000   =   3.0

Remember that current assets are turned into cash generally within 12 months, while current liabilities represent obligations that must be paid within the same 12 months. A financially healthy company will have more than enough current asset value to cover payments of its current liabilities. A current ratio of 2.0 or higher is desirable, although a somewhat lower current ratio might still be considered healthy for a company of high liquidity if current assets are mostly cash or if the business is cash-oriented. A ratio that is too high, however, can be a sign of problems. A ratio of more than 5.0, for example, tells you that the current assets of the company are more than five times its current liabilities. This could be an indication that business volume is not meeting expectations—the company is not able to sell its products—or that the company is not using its assets to best advantage. For example, it might be holding cash instead of investing in new product development or advertising. XYZ's current ratio of 3.0 means that it has three times as many current assets (which will be turned to cash through business operations over the next 12 months) as current liabilities (debts to be paid off in the next 12 months). XYZ should have no trouble meeting its obligations.

Another important current relationship is the ratio of cash and equivalents (that is, assets that can easily be converted into cash, such as marketable securities) to current liabilities. This is sometimes called the *acid-test ratio*.

Some current assets are more difficult to turn into cash than others. For example, it may take months to turn inventories into cash to cover current obligations. The acid-test ratio calculates the amount of cash and marketable securities (which can readily be converted to cash) a company has to cover its current liabilities.

cash   + marketable securities ÷ current liabilities = acid-test ratio

$38,000 + $200,000   ÷ $316,000   =   75%

Capital Structure   The capitalization, or *capital structure*, is the total amount of money invested in a company. This amount includes both bonds (long-term debt) and equity (money paid by investors to the company). The capital structure is calculated from information on the company's balance sheet. For XYZ, it would be figured this way:

Long-term debt	$ 85,000	7%
Stockholders' equity	1,150,000	93%
Total capitalization	$1,235,000	100%

Note that the total capitalization is always 100 percent.

     Understanding a company's capitalization structure is one of the most important ways to determine how risky a particular company's stock is as an investment. In the case of XYZ, we see that only a small percentage of its total capitalization consists of long-term debt. Most of the money invested in the company has not come from borrowing but from stockholders who bought the company's stock and from the company's own earnings. (Remember, any profits the company does not distribute to shareholders in dividends is added to stockholders' equity as retained earnings.) In the investment world, this type of capital structure is considered to be quite conservative and risk-free because the company owes very little money to such outsiders as banks and bondholders. It will pay very little in interest expenses because it carries so little debt.

Companies with more aggressive financial management may borrow more money from banks to finance their growth and expansion. The capitalization table of such a company may show a long-term debt of 40 percent or higher. This would be a riskier investment because the company would be required to pay more in interest costs (because of its greater debt) and eventually repay the borrowed money as well. Higher interest payments would, of course, come out of earnings. A company that goes into debt to finance growth is, of course, hoping for greater earnings and profitability in the future. A company would borrow money instead of relying on its own earnings as XYZ does because management believes it can expand more quickly and increase sales, thus earning more money than the cost of borrowing. Borrowing gives a company flexibility to take advantage of opportunities for growth.

Cash Flow   *Cash flow*, the actual amount of money that is available to the company for operations, is figured from information on the source and application of funds statement. Remember from our discussion of the sources and uses statement that depreciation can be considered a source of funds. For this reason, depreciation can be added back into the company's net income to figure out how much cash the company actually earned during the year:

net income + depreciation = cash flow

$184,000 + $69,000 = $253,000

Earnings Per Share   The *earnings per share* figure is probably watched more closely by the financial community than any other company statistic. This figure is obtained by dividing net earnings (from the income statement) by

A container ship transports U.S. products to foreign countries. If the dollar loses value in terms of foreign currency, companies that sell abroad face loss of revenues even when sales are high.

the number of shares outstanding. Using the XYZ Company as an example, net earnings for last year were $184,000 and the company had 200,000 shares of stock outstanding. Earnings per share would be $.92.

The number of shares outstanding may change during the year. A company may issue more shares of stock to raise equity capital, or it may buy back some of its outstanding shares. If the number of shares outstanding changes, earnings per share are calculated based on the average number of shares outstanding during the year rather than the number outstanding at year end.

Earnings per share can also be calculated in a way that illustrates a relationship between the various financial statements of the company:

book value per share × return on equity = earnings per share

$5.75   ×   16%   = $.92

(Find the calculations for book value on page 27 and for return on equity on page 30.)

Analyzing Sales

Achieving a high profit return on the stockholders' investment is of prime importance to the company's management. As additional money is invested in the business (either in the form of new capital or reinvested earnings), sales should increase. Sales growth is important in itself, but it has little meaning if each additional dollar of sales does not produce the profit to justify the new investment. For these reasons, investors should watch for trends in sales, profit margins, and return on equity.

Monitoring Sales Growth An increase or decrease in sales can occur in any or all of these three ways:

1. An increase or decline in the absolute number of units sold by the company. If a company generates $2 million of sales each year by selling 2,000 units for $1,000 each ($1,000 × 2,000 = $2,000,000), an increase of 200 units sold would add $200,000 to total sales ($1,000 × 200 = $200,000).
2. Raising or lowering the selling price of each unit. By raising the selling price of its products, a company can increase its total sales, assuming that the total number of units sold remains the same. If the company in the above example raised the price of its products from $1,000 to $1,100 but continued to sell 2,000 units, it would increase sales to $2.2 million. This is the same result that would be achieved by increasing the number of units sold from 2,000 to 2,200 at the original price.
3. For a company that sells its products in a foreign market, an increase or decline in the exchange rate of the dollar for another country's currency will have the same effect of raising or lowering the price per unit. For example, if a U.S. company sold its products in France

for francs and the value of the dollar declined so that fewer francs would be equivalent to the dollar, the company would need to sell more units of its product to earn the same amount in dollars.

A close reading of the company's financial statements, including notes, will tell investors whether any of these factors affected revenues from sales in the previous year.

Equity Turnover Another effective method of measuring a company's sales progress is watching for a trend in *equity turnover*. This is determined by dividing sales by the average stockholders' equity (total revenues, $2,252,000 ÷ equity, $1,150,000). The level of equity turnover often reflects the type of business in which the company is engaged. As a general rule, companies in industries with high profit margins have a low equity turnover, whereas companies in low profitability industries have a high equity turnover. A trend, either up or down, could be important for investors to consider.

A company can improve its return on equity either by increasing its equity turnover or its profitability or both, as the following formula indicates, again using XYZ as an example:

equity turnover × net profit margin = return on equity

2.0　　　×　　8%　　=　　16%

For XYZ to improve its return on equity to 18 percent from 16 percent, management would either have to achieve a net profit margin closer to 9 percent or increase the equity turnover to more than 2.2, or a combination of both.

Return on equity is not the same for every industry, as the table on page 30 illustrates. In recent years, the average return on equity for major industries in the United States has been just over 13 percent.

The rapidly expanding computer field exemplifies a growth industry.

Growth and Basic Industries

Basic industries, such as steel manufacturing, offer generally stable and predictable sales and earnings.

Some industries are regarded as growth industries, while others are referred to as basic industries. In general, *growth industries* are those with dramatically increasing sales and profitability. For example, computer manufacturing has been a growth industry since the first computers were introduced for industrial use in the 1960s. Sales and profits have grown by leaps and bounds each year, especially in the 1980s, when the introduction of personal computers expanded the market to small businesses, schools, and households. Investors typically expect growth industries to have superior profitability. *Basic industries*, on the other hand, have been around for a while and are not expected to demonstrate enormous growth in sales and earnings. They are, rather, expected to continue at a steady, relatively stable rate. Typical basic industries are steel, paper, and shoe manufacturing. Investors look to basic industries for stability and predictability. Investors should realize, of course, that within every industry some companies are more profitable than others.

GLOSSARY

accounts payable Money owed by a company to short-term creditors, such as suppliers.

accounts receivable Money owed to a company by its customers.

acid-test ratio The relationship of liquid assets (cash and equivalents) to current liabilities.

assets Everything that a company owns, including what is owed to it. Assets can include cash, equipment, patents, or receivables.

auditor's report A report issued by an independent accounting firm attesting to the correct preparation and accuracy of a corporation's financial statements.

balance sheet A statement of a company's assets and liabilities at the end of the fiscal year.

basic industry An area of industry generally involving established companies that produce essential products, in which sales are steady and predictable, and profits stable.

book value The amount of equity behind a share of common stock, calculated by dividing the net worth of a company by the number of shares of stock outstanding.

capitalization or **capital structure** The amount of money invested in a company; the value realized by a company from the sale of its securities.

cash flow The actual money derived from operations that is available for company expenditures.

current ratio The relationship of current assets to current liabilities.

depreciation The decline in value of a capital asset over a period of time.

earnings, net earnings, or **net profit** A company's total revenues minus its costs, expenses, and taxes.

earnings per share A company's net profit divided by the number of shares of stock owned.

equity turnover Total sales divided by the average stockholders' equity. In general, companies in industries with high profit margins have low equity turnover, and vice versa.

gross profits Total revenues from sales minus the cost of sales as shown in a company's income statement; also referred to as gross income or gross earnings.

growth industry An area of industry generally involving new and developing products that is characterized by increasing sales and profitability.

income statement A record of a company's business results for the year, specifying sales, costs, and earnings.

inventory Raw materials, supplies, work in process, and finished products that are considered to be part of a company's current assets.

liabilities Debts, payments due to suppliers, salaries due to employees, and anything else that a company owes.

negative working capital The lack of operating funds available when current liabilities exceed current assets.

net profit margin A measure of the company's profitability after costs, expenses, and taxes.

operating profit margin A comparison of before-tax profits to income from sales.

par value The stated amount of a stock or face value of a bond.

preferred stock Stock that has a priority claim on assets, dividends, and earnings.

pretax profit margin A company's profits calculated before taxes have been subtracted.

profit margin The percentage of a company's sales that become profits.

prospectus The official public report of a company that must be given to potential buyers of a newly issued stock.

proxy statement A statement, mailed to stockholders before an annual or special meeting, containing information about the election of officers and other issues pertaining to the company.

retained earnings Profits that are not distributed to stockholders but are used to operate the company.

retention rate The percentage of a company's net earnings that is reinvested in the business instead of being paid out to investors.

securities An investment such as stocks, bonds, and options.

securities analyst A person who researches the companies issuing stocks and bonds to assess their future potential and make trading recommendations.

source and application of funds statement A record of changes in a company's financial position over the past year, detailing where operating funds for the company originated and how the company made its money.

stockholders' equity The net worth of a company; the value of a company's assets minus its debts and obligations.

working capital The amount of money that a firm can actually use in its operations for the next year; current assets minus current liabilities.

FURTHER READING

Business Week, published by McGraw-Hill, Inc. Weekly magazine providing thorough news coverage of the business world, including features on various types of companies and investment-related topics.

Handbook of OTC Stocks and *Handbook of Common Stocks*, published by Moody's Investors Service, provide overviews of the businesses of more than 2,000 companies, including per share data and other statistics for 7 or more years.

Inc., Published by Inc. Publishing Corporation. Contains feature articles about new and growing companies and their managers as well as regular columns that provide insight into the development of a company.

New York Stock Exchange Stock Reports, American Stock Exchange Stock Reports, and *Over-the-Counter Stock Reports*, published by Standard & Poor's, contain periodically revised 2-page surveys of thousands of companies, including the latest stock prices, the current year's range, a 7-year chart of high and low prices, earnings and dividend rankings, and summaries of the company's financial data.

INDEX